Flowers *Silk*

FAUX FLORAL ARRANGEMENTS
FOR CONTEMPORARY LIVING

Camilla Svensson Burns

APPLE

A Quintet Book

First published in the UK in 2007 by
Apple Press
7 Greenland Street
London NW1 0ND
www.apple-press.com

ISBN: 978-1-84543-227-0

This book was designed and produced by
Quintet Publishing Limited
6 Blundell Street
London N7 9BH

Publisher: Gaynor Sermon
Senior Editor: Marian Broderick
Project Editor: Katy Bevan
Photography: Allyson Magda
Design: Dean Martin, Jason Anscomb

10 9 8 7 6 5 4 3 2 1
Colour separation by Pica Digital Pte Ltd.
Printed in Singapore by Star Standard Industries Ltd

Flowers

Contents

Introduction.........................6

Materials and design 10

Colour and mood................28

Seasons and holidays 52

Outside-in 78

Occasions 100

Stockists 126

Index 127

Welcome to the world of faux florals

Working with silks and dried materials raises many paradoxes: The ease of not having to go to the flower market at three in the morning and then conditioning the flowers is equally offset by the challenge of finding really true replications of natural beauty. Both materials need some alterations to fit into your vision.

Fresh flowers may need the stems cut or a couple of leaves pruned and this is, for the most part, pretty easily done with a sharp knife or scissors. Contrary to what you might think, silks need a bit of muscle. (I advise investing in some really good cutting tools; you can read more about this in the *essential equipment* section on page 14.) With fresh flowers you have to work with what you get. This can be both a challenge and an adventure. Who knows how many hours are spent wandering the flower market stalls or walking through orchards just to find the precise and perfectly curving branch or orchid stem. Silks make this a lot easier. You can defy the limits of nature and manipulate the stems and petals to give you exactly what you want, and with the power of the almighty glue gun, the creations are endless. And the most obvious, while you may miss out on the magical transformation of an opening bloom, the release of fragrance over the days, or the casual relaxation of the stems and leaves as they settle into new shapes or surprise you with one last growth spurt: silk flowers won't wither and die after a few days.

Silks have come a long way over the past few years. The line between imitation and fresh has been blurred by the pursuit of perfection. Often people ask if an arrangement is real and vice versa. A lot of the "natural" appearance is owed to the artists that make the silk materials, but that's only part of the equation. It's up to you and your experience and experimentation to give

your arrangements the attention to detail that will set them apart. I guarantee that when you really hit a design on the head, you'll fool people and the comments of "Is that real?" will never cease to bring a smile to your face.

One of the most important guiding principles of floral design is to enjoy yourself. I try to incorporate some fun into every arrangement that I do. Sometimes this will be a playful approach to design that any observer will notice, other times it might be very subtle, like mixing up flowers that don't traditionally *pair well* or couldn't possibly be found together in nature. For example, try cutting off some orchid blooms and gluing them onto a willow branch. It's fun like this that keeps things, er, fresh.

This is not intended to be the definitive book on silk floral design. I see it as merely a chance for you to get inspired by what you are truly capable of. If you like some of the designs found here enough to copy, then I am truly flattered. But let me challenge you to venture on your own and play with things. Have some fun and experiment. Maybe you'll find that where I used a daffodil, you might prefer a daisy. You might think that raspberries in a winter wreath are crazy, but if substituting them with cranberries makes you smile—then go for it. Enjoy the process and look outside the box for inspiration. Don't be afraid to try new things or defy convention. But most importantly, have fun!

Camilla Svensson Burns

Materials and design

This introductory section will guide you through the basic tools and materials you'll need along with some essential advice to get you started. You'll find a quick guide to faux flowers and how to look after them, useful accessories and container examples that complement your arrangements. A simple overview of colour and design form will give you further insight into flower arranging, and perhaps inspire you to explore further.

Permanent botanicals

Artificial and dried flowers are referred to collectively as "permanent botanicals" or otherwise, "silks." Faux flowers originated in China and were actually made of silk and used to decorate hairpieces, clothing and costumes, eventually making their way to plant arrangements. Very few are actually made of silk any more and are now made primarily of synthetic materials.

The Italians were said to have used silk from cocoons to create silk flowers and the French soon followed. It is said that when a silk rose bud was presented to Marie Antoinette, in 1775, she was so enamored by the beauty of the bloom that she fainted. After the French Revolution, many of the artisans who made silks were displaced and made their way to England and eventually America.

The Victorian period elevated flowers to an almost cult status and gave us an entire period where almost everything was decorated in flowers. By the 1800s all sorts of materials were being used to manufacture flowers. Satin, muslin, calico, velvet, crepe and gauze were just a few of the popular fabrics. Flowers were even made out of wax and human hair to commemorate the death of a loved one.

TECHNICAL DEVELOPMENTS

Materials for silks became more refined as manufacturing processes became more specialized in the mid 1900s. In the 1940s, Japan, which was making flowers out of celluloid, was banned from importing flowers to the United States after numerous disastrous fires had been linked to its use. In the 1970s, Asia, namely China, became the prominent source for silks. Unfortunately the boom that they initially enjoyed was quickly squelched as quality control and a flood of cheap imitations saturated the market.

Standard manufacturing materials today include paper, parchment, cotton, plastic, and rubber. For higher quality artificial flowers, silk is still used as well as rayon and cotton. The petals may also be coated with thin layers of latex to give a more realistic sheen and texture to resemble its real-life inspiration. You will also sometimes find real dried materials worked into arrangements. Often on tree and plant based items real sticks, twigs, berries, and branches are used to add to the realism.

GREEN FINGERS

Today, silks are making a comeback. With global concerns about pesticides and the rising price of energy, it's become more expensive to get fresh flowers. Coupled with busy schedules and the social pressure to "go green," increasingly people are turning to permanent botanicals. The quality of flowers is better than ever and they are so lifelike that it's difficult to tell some arrangements from the real thing without close inspection.

MAINTENANCE

Silk and dried flowers will require some cleaning and care just like any other item of beauty. For starters, it's best to keep silks out of direct sunlight as it may cause some to fade or become brittle. This simple practice is really not that much different from what you would do with cut flowers, so it shouldn't be a problem. Second, since you are going to have silks around for a long time they will inherently get dusty. Your best defence is to add them to your regular cleaning regime. A simple dusting with a feather duster should do the trick to keep most surface dust off of them. Another method to get to the dirt that gets into deeper crevices is to used compressed air. You can purchase bottles of compressed air in a can, like they use for dusting photography and computer equipment, which is available at most related stores. If you are going to vacuum, place a screening device such as some stretched tights over the nozzle in case you dislodge a leaf or stamen.

DEEP CLEANING

Another method of deep cleaning is to either wipe down all of the leaves with a slightly damp cloth, or to submerge the flowers in some slightly soapy water. This last method is best reserved for plants, greens and latex coated flowers as the water might ruin the structure or colour of non-coated leaves. Test a small leaf first before trying this method. The other downside is that you will have to take apart and rebuild your arrangement after it is cleaned if you use the wet method.

Finally, there are some products on the market for cleaning silk and dried flowers. In actuality, they don't really clean, they just coat the leaves and their dust and add shine via chemicals. They can make your shiny leaves and petals look great, but at some point you will have to wipe them down anyway.

Essential equipment

Very few tools are required to work with permanent flowers. The bare essentials are cutting tools and attaching devices. Most of the equipment you need is available through good craft shops and industry outlets. The internet is also an invaluable resource in finding specific or elusive items.

TOOLS

1. Bolt cutters
2. Good-quality scissors
3. Wire cutters
4. Sharp knife
5. Glue gun

Clockwise from right: A collection of ribbons; florist's tape, wire, stakes and staples; foam bases in a variety of shapes.

CUTTING

Most silk flowers and flora have wire inside their stems, so you are going to be doing some strenuous cutting. It is advisable to invest in a pair of very good wire cutters and a pair of small bolt cutters for thicker stems. The higher-quality tools will save your hands from blisters and your wrists from arthritis. Additionally, a sharp pair of scissors is necessary—clean cuts on ribbons are imperative for neatness as well as to avoid fraying.

FIXING

Various tools and methods will help you with all of the attaching you will be doing. Using a hot glue gun will save you time and enable you to add an item without having to wire it in. Other projects will require you to use wire: add several gauges and lengths to your inventory of supplies. Another useful tool is the floral pick. These little guys are great to extend or create stems; however kebab skewers or toothpicks can work just as well.

You will need florists tape to attach some materials. Get a couple of widths and types to work with. You'll find that flat matte paper-tape will blend nicely into the base of buds if needed but the holding strength of green nylon tape has advantages as well.

FOAM

These integral blocks are the foundation for many arrangements. Dry foam or Styrofoam is essential when arranging a more complicated design; it enables you to create a permanent or temporary support structure with the help of hot glue. Dry foam is a lot like wet foam but it is more rigid and does not soak up water like the wet-type of floral foam or oasis. If you are in a bind though, you can definitely use wet foam for your arrangement.

EMBELLISHMENTS

Ribbon can be a huge design element, especially with bouquets and wedding décor. It is worth having a variety of colours, widths, patterns, and textured ribbon in your stash, so that you know you always have something to choose from when embarking on a new project.

EXTRAS

There are many new products becoming available all the time, some of which you may find useful. You can mist your flowers with scents that are specifically designed for permanent florals, or even use fake water droplets to give that fresh from the garden look. One useful addition

Accessories

Having a house and studio full of knickknacks that can be pulled out to add drama and dimension to an arrangement is great—a florist can never have enough accessories. Use fruit and vegetables, or play with whatever is in season, or if you need a lift on a rainy day, bring out a bowl of faux cherries to make you smile. Moss, pebbles, and shells are the norm, but how about some different kinds of displays: sprouting twig balls in a pair of wrought iron urns in the hallway; an old wooden trough holding spheres of moss in all different sizes displayed on a dinner table; dogwood branches splaying out of a garden urn placed upon an antique cabinet…

Clockwise from top left: Twig balls; branches add height; glass balls and marbles; moss balls; pebbles for weight and texture.

Opposite: Fruit and vegetables can be real or imitation.

TWIG AND MOSS BALLS

These are pretty easy to find at craft stores and garden centres. Twig balls are usually made out of willow or dried vines and are helpful for keeping stems upright. Both would make great temporary filler for a large container that is waiting for your next arrangement. You can make these on your own with a little perseverance.

MOSS

A definite staple for designers, moss is very versatile. You can use it to cover and hide the mechanics of your work, and as a filler. Or you can use it as a focal component that adds texture and colour.

BRANCHES

Twigs of all shapes and sizes and colours are one of the most versatile accessories you can have. Best of all, they don't need to cost a thing! Branches can add height, complement dimension, create visual interest, and can be formed into shapes and designs. One favourite trick is to glue the blooms from orchids onto curly willow.

FRUIT AND VEGETABLES

Organic matter can be used just for the sake of its colour or shape, ignoring what it actually is: A lime can be sometimes just an oval or a colour accent. Artichokes are so fun to use and always get a great response once people discover them hidden away in a design. Play with your use of fruit and vegetables—try stacking them, gluing them in patterns, or using cut fruits or real dried examples.

PEBBLES AND STONES

These serve a dual purpose. They make great ornamental filler that can add colour and texture inside a glass vase or filling the brim of a container. You can also use them as ballast at the bottom of a container when you need to counterbalance a tall or top-heavy structure. Find pebbles in nature rather than using manufactured stones or machine-polished varieties.

MARBLES AND BAUBLES

While glass marbles may be similar to the features of pebbles and stones they can also be more elegant. These two items seem a bit more deliberate, and their use and placement is usually done with care, especially the larger baubles. If a vase seems empty, try adding either one to add new dimension to an arrangement.

Design styles and principles

Clockwise from below: This oversized
tea-cup is a humorous choice for
a child's party; symmetrical display
in a square container; informal but
traditional topiary; natural flower
heads; cascading greenery.

Showing flowers off in their simplest form is often the most successful approach. Explore and experience the possibilities—the end result should be harmonious and easy on the eye. There are certain "rules" specific to floral design, but you do not necessarily have to follow them: a designer must have freedom after all. So, without going too far into design fundamentals, let's touch on the basics.

NATURAL

An organic approach to design allows flowers to do what they want to do naturally and should reflect how they grow in nature. This can be challenging to emulate when working with permanent flowers, as they need to be manipulated into a natural "bend." You can practise your technique by imitating the shape and imperfections of a fresh flower with a silk copy.

ARTISTIC

You can make a deliberate statement by emulating the feel of an artistic style. To follow a set of standards or textbook rules is not creating art; it's just copying. Rules are meant to be broken—break away from tradition and impart your own interpretation.

RIGID

No one wants to be thought of as being inflexible. However, a touch of "rigidity" can be useful as a supporting element. A stiff grass might make a perfect backdrop or help to frame a subject flower. Rigid design as an artistic interpretation is best left to those who love it.

CASCADING

A flowing arrangement is most appealing when it cascades like a waterfall. It is possible to wire, or glue, flowers into a cascade-like position, but then it can become very stiff. With real flowers you might have to follow the direction that a branch of vine wants to flow in. This can be a challenge as flowers and stems want to do their own thing. With silks, you can manipulate the stems to do what you want, and then the challenge becomes to make it look life-like. Take a hint from nature, and try to ease the longer stems into a bend rather than forming a hard angle. Take a walk into your garden or look at photographs to see how gracefully things flow.

BUNCHING

This is grouping the same type of flower or colour group into a mass for greater visual impact. This is one of my favourite methods for creating bouquets. In arrangements, this technique can be used to your advantage when you have a limited number of colours or variety of flowers to work with. Bunching will draw the eye to the mass and create more of an impression than randomly scattered flowers that might otherwise get lost.

Colour concepts

Advances in manufacturing have allowed faux florals to catch up with some of the latest colourways and variations that the fresh flower world has to offer. One guiding influence in the matter of colour is fashion and design. Industry and consumer magazines will usually let you know what colours are going to be "in" for the season before you see them on the street. Let's face it, the mavericks of the fashion world have more influence on what will be the hottest autumn colours than the winner of the next Chelsea Flower Show.

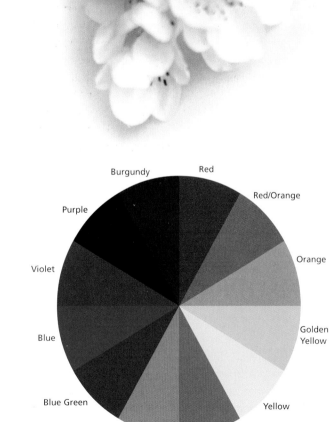

MONOCHROMATIC

A monochrome style uses only a combination of tints, shades and hues of one colour. By combining different tones of one colour, you can create dimension and texture since not all flowers or foliage have the same shape, sheen and hue. This method yields sophisticated and uncluttered designs. It truly shows off the beauty of the flora and foliage without over doing it with lots of colour combinations and variety. If you try to work with too many colour combinations they all get lost as they compete for attention.

COMPLEMENTARY COLOURS

Try to limit your palette to one or two complementary hues. The idea of using colours that vibrate against each other is also thrilling. Combinations like orange and chocolate brown, or shocking pink and purple with lavender accents, are exciting and eye catching. If all else fails you can always resort to an artists colour wheel (see opposite). This tried and true method of showing which colours match and complement each other can guide you if you are in any doubt. To find the complemetary, pick the colour opposite to your main choice.

CAPTURE THE FEELING

Designs can be guided by feeling and mood. Colour can really alter one's outlook, for example, the "Bowl of Sunshine" arrangement is undeniably happy. I once worked on a wedding and the reception was being held in a very dark restaurant, so to bring light and life into the space, I filled glass bowls with lemons and a plethora of frilly white parrot tulips. Combined with candlelight and the happy couple, it became a wonderful and bright evening reception.

On the flip side, maybe you want to create an opulent atmosphere with dark, inky colours. Many clients ask for a sophisticated design of garnets, ruby reds, chocolate brown and even "black" flowers. These are available as black baccarat roses and black calla lilies, plum tree foliage in rich burgundy and smoke bush leaves in chocolate.

THIS SEASON'S FASHION

One other hint for colour selection is to emulate the colours of the season. Spring—pastel and soft. Summer—vibrant and crisp. Autumn —rich and warm. Winter—moody and opulent. There is definitely a correlation between the two: whenever a colour is fashionable, it becomes the rage in flower colours for a couple of seasons at a time.

MOOD BOARDS

A great way to find out which colours are at the cutting edge is to look at design resources, especially fashion and interior decorator magazines. As a designer, it is imperative to know the latest trends, the hottest colours and most popular looks, and research through these sources can be fruitful. A great way to gather colour information, especially when planning a wedding or party, is to collect paint chips from a hardware store, ribbon and magazine cuttings.

Being inspired by the most trivial things can end up being the most powerful element in a design. On one of my photo shoots for *Your Wedding Day* magazine, my inspiration for the whole table setting was an heirloom tomato. The tomato was so beautiful with its sunset coloured variegation that I went out and bought all sorts of fabulous fabrics and wonderful flowers to complement the tomatoes featured in the article.

Above: The inspirational heirloom tomato; **Left:** Autumn hues; **Facing page, clockwise from top left:** Silk orchids, Lift the mood with bright colours; Complementary colours in arrangement; Colour wheel.

Choosing a container

As with most elements of design, there are basic concepts to learn when choosing a container—what some people call the correct process. When an artist paints they may choose to use a canvas or type of paper that will best reflect their work. But we all know what fun can result when they go off the beaten path. Choosing a container is similar. There are certain basic guidelines to follow like weight, colour, and shape relative to the mass of your project, but don't confine yourself too much.

Containers are a big part of the success of an arrangement and should complement the size and shape of the flowers or foliage. Almost anything can become a vessel to arrange in, as we are working with permanent materials, so they need not be watertight. Why not try some of the following: a collection of teacups, old pitchers and jugs, contemporary wooden boxes, cigar boxes, baskets, silk lanterns in all shapes and sizes, galvanized buckets and pails, antique apple crates, garden urns, trophy cups, tall and bulbous apothecary jars, soup terrines, you name it.

Clockwise from top left: Baskets; ceramics pots; urns; glass vases; boxes.

Opposite: Old and new silver; an antique collection.

BASKETS

As one of the oldest vessels known to man, baskets come in all shapes and sizes. You will find a tremendous variety in the colours and weaves of baskets depending on the culture they originate from. One can easily give an arrangement a cultural flair just by using a particular basket. Have some fun and try using non-traditional baskets made out of wire or twigs.

CERAMICS

These come in all sorts of fun and funky colours and designs—definitely a staple to have in your collection. Ceramics are useful because of their weight and durability. Having cupboards filled with them may drive your partner nuts, but be assured, you will use them all the time. Try changing arrangements into different coloured and shaped containers, it will freshen up a space or can pull a room's colour scheme together. These are great flea-market or impulse buys. Don't be afraid to pick something up just because the colour intrigues you. You'll be sure to use it sometime.

BOXES

A big benefit of using a dry medium is the advantage of not needing the container to be watertight. You can easily notice that these boxes would most likely not be water tight, and yet they hold flowers. The contradiction only adds to the style and shows confidence from the designer.

GLASS

Transparent vessels become tricky with silks because of the expectation for water to fill them. People have become so accustomed to seeing flowers in water that in most cases, a glass vase with dry stems leaves the viewer unsettled. It doesn't bother me and in fact, I often will place some curly willow or old branches with moss on them in a giant glass vase or apothecary jar. Make sure that your stems are of equal quality to the flowers. Sometimes you will find a nice looking bloom is mated to an unrealistic stem and this will just detract from your display. If you really want the water look then you can use an acrylic product called Aqua Clear that will set crystal clear and looks just like fresh water.

URNS

Urns, Urns, Urns! You can get these in all shapes and sizes and made out of all types of materials, but cast iron ones are a favourite. There is a heft and girth about them that not only makes a statement, but the solid base gives you almost limitless design possibilities for larger, and taller, arrangements. They can be heavy, so work with them on a rotating coaster and if large, try to work on the arrangement near to where it will ultimately be placed.

SILVER

What better colour than silver to give an arrangement a touch of class or define its elegance. I get a kick out of using old trophy cups and chalices that I find in thrift stores. They may have engravings or names on them but what fun, and a great conversation piece, to find a really old one with an engraving from 100 years ago.

ANTIQUE

Distressed, shabby-chic, patina, accelerated aging, whatever you want to call it: I call it character. Leave old metal baskets and candelabras outside year round in order to weather them. If you ever need to dress down, or freshen up, the look of an arrangement, try an old container—you might just get something new.

The artist's palette

Selecting flowers and foliage is about the adventure. With permanent florals, choices can be guided more by creative forces than by formulas and definitions about what each flower is supposed to symbolize and when it is supposed to be used. You have to think about the physical aspects of a flower or green if it's fresh. With silks you have a big advantage because you can always manipulate the foliage into a form that you can work with—glue can do wonders. You don't have to worry about whether a hydrangea will wilt in the heat or if something is available in January. You have the advantage of being able to get whatever flower in whatever colour you want year round. The added bonus is that there is a wire stem in the middle so you can bend it in any direction you want.

Choose flowers by colour, texture, and character. If you are looking for a yellow themed arrangement, find the best yellows you can and then determine if the feel of the arrangement needs to be serious, flamboyant, whimsical, or whatever. If you want a light and airy look, choose petite blooms from forsythia branches. For a more elegant look go with orchids. If you need whimsy, some daffodils or kangaroo paws might be the choice.

Texture is equally important. Smooth, sultry shapes evoke a very different feel to pointy petals; large, shiny leaves to a leather leaf fern. Texture adds drama and interest to an arrangement much like a great painting that keeps your eye constantly moving around it.

Fantastic foliage
Shape, structure, and balance: foliage adds texture and dimension.
Fern frond, onion grass, echevaria, jade, lambs-ear, coriander, ruscus, green berries, wild grass, philodendron xanadu, maiden hair fern, strelitzia, umbrella fern.

Tropical allure
Fresh and crisp, bold angular lines of the leaves and stems, vivid and bright colours, never-ending variety of fascinating shapes, sizes, and colour.
Antherium, fiddlehead fern, ginger, pineapple lily, pincushion protea.

Bluebell fields

Delft blue, sky blue, ice blue... what comes to mind when using this palette is cool water, serene and delicate.

Light and dark blue delphinium, lavender, agapanthus.

Sahara sunset

Brilliant oranges, saturated gold, and golden papaya evoke warmth; daring and playful.

Dahlia, banksia rose, hypericum berry, poppy, rosehip, tulip, columbine, cymbidium orchid, garden rose.

Imperial purple

Inky, dusky, and sultry magenta. Purple brings to mind rich and magnificent compositions.

Anemone, cornflower, pansy, muscari.

Deep pinks

Dark coral pink, vivid, and glowing; pink brings a glorious splash of colour to an arrangement. Happy and frivolous, the most requested colour in the flower world.

Calla lily, coxcomb, raspberry, anemone, garden rose, cherries, spider gerbera.

Sunshine delight

Sunny, egg yolk, and citrus yellow, add fresh vibrancy to a late spring gathering.

Ranunculus, oncidium orchid, sunflower, daffodil, forsythia.

Pink passion

Delicious shades of sorbet, translucent shades of pink. Subtle and beautiful, pale pink is one the most popular colours for a springtime bride.

Poke berry, tulip, glorious lily, rubrum lily, floribunda garden rose, peony, tulip, peony bud.

Earthy tones

Cool, tawny browns and the colours of earth, sepia and umber: all natural shades found in the landscape surrounding us.

Olive branch, chocolate sunflower, sunflower bud, pepper berry, twigs, pod burst, mahogany echevaria.

Jewel tones

Opulent garnet, crimson, and ruby; passionate, sensual and romantic, colours associated with Christmas and Valentine's day.

Rose, amaryllis, asiatic lily, fritillaries.

Creamy, buttery pastels

Pale straw, warm creams, and buttery shades of ivory. Restful and incredibly elegant when used as one, or a mix, of varying hues.

Mistletoe, pear blossom, casablanca, English rose, camellia, lotus flower, dahlia, hydrangea, lily of the valley.

Settings and design influences

The setting in which you display your flowers, or are given to work with, can make all the difference to your approach. The flowers you choose, the container, the size, and style of the design will all be influenced by the surroundings. As a general rule you should respect the inherent qualities of the environment in which you are working. And if there are none—well, then you can have a ball and go wild.

In addition to settings, a person's style or a season can influence the design and choice of flora. A petite bride would probably not do too well with a long, flowing bouquet half her size, just as a sunflower might look awkward in a winter display. On the other hand, juxtaposition can help an arrangement stand out by making a statement through contrast, like crystal chandeliers in an old wooden barn. And what fun to bring in cool and swanky oversized glass vases with submerged stems of orchids or tropical leaves to a black-tie event that normally calls for stuffy rose arrangements.

What you end up doing is ultimately going to be what feels comfortable to you. Everyone will benefit from learning the basic principles of design, but it's what you do with what you learn that is important. It's hard to learn style and taste and much easier to mimic trends and follow fashion. Look at yourself and honestly evaluate where you stand. Can you pull off your own style with confidence or are you better suited to imitate? Neither is right or wrong, but knowing what you are best at will allow you to know where to spend your energy.

SEASONS

— Autumn: Crab apples and twigs, berries, brambling vines.
— Winter: Dark colours, holiday themes.
— Spring: Fresh shades, crisp green foliage.
— Summer: Bright blooms and colour combinations.

CONSERVATIVE

Heavy crystal, elegant vases with traditional styles, and symmetry all work well in a conservative home or setting. Lilies, roses and magnolia can all be formal if designed with structure in mind.

COSMOPOLITAN

Clear vases, jewels, repetition, clean, modern design, possibly more line forms or artistic statements like a giant collection of cut rose heads in a large flat container in a pavé style used as a centrepiece.

RUSTIC

For this shabby-chic style think of weather worn containers found in an old barn. Heavy wrought iron candelabra with textured flora and foliage, such as antique hydrangea florets mixed with smoke bush leaves, floribunda roses and hanging amaranths.

COTTAGE

For the country cottage look choose antique vessels with garden cuttings. Old buckets and milk churns, or mossy terracotta pots, brimming over with lavender, honeysuckle vines, ladies mantle and hollyhocks.

Opposite: This symmetrical table setting adds a romantic formality to the outdoor setting.

Above: Pebbles and seashells were used to create an exotic beach theme for this party. The monochrome scheme using simple glass and only natural tones help the effect.

Colour and mood

In this section we look at arrangements that capture an atmosphere, or evoke a feeling, acheiving drama or calmness through the use of colour and choice of materials. Colours can be hot and vivid, dark and mysterious, or in combination, any mood that you choose. With no limit to the choice of flora due to seasonality, you are free to pursue any impression or feeling you wish to evoke with the use of colour.

Cherry red

MATERIALS

1. Scarlet garden roses x 12
2. Vivid pink spider gerbera daisies x 7
3. Fuzzy wuzzy coxscomb with leaves x 5
4. Hot pink French anemonies x 10
5. Cherry red cherries to fill
6. Dry foam
7. Florist's tape
8. Plastic floral foam dish
9. Tall glass vase

Racy, exciting, sexy: This arrangement is not for the meek. If you want to make a statement, you have to go bold. When using big, bright, and powerful colours, gather them en masse, if you don't they can get lost or work against your colour scheme and break up the harmony.

1 Cut your foam to fit the plastic dish and secure with tape.

2 Fill your vase two-thirds full with the cherries and nestle the dish into the vase on top so the sides are concealed.

3 Insert roses into the foam and arrange loosely to mimic nature.

4 Add the anemones and gerbera in groupings to create impact.

By using only deep reds, this
arrangement is bold and strong.

5 When cutting the stems of the coxscomb,
save the remaining stems with leaves as filler
to be used in step 7.

6 Insert the texturally complex coxcomb
so that is slightly taller than its neighbouring
flowers either side.

7 Tuck in the saved coxcomb stems
intermittently for fabulous colour contrast.

Mellow colours in an old-world urn

Inspired by vineyards and olive groves, with their changing colours and contrasting textures, this arrangement represents the new growth of flora and the mature vines and aged trees. The crisp white lilies and celery-green buds stand out against the tawny browns and earth, sepia, and umber colours characteristic of the vines and their flora. This arrangement would make a perfect centrepiece for a Tuscan-themed dinner party, or placed on top of an antique dresser.

1 Set dry foam into a base container, tape into place, put into the urn, and surround with dry moss to conceal.

2 Starting with the lily, arrange the longer stems toward the centre, with smaller heads and buds leaning over the edge. Next, add the iris to establish the basic design. Fill in with helleborus and safari sunset, arranging them in groups for impact. Rotate the arrangement constantly so that it looks good when viewed from all sides.

3 To create visual texture, cut the roses to different lengths, and add in clusters—tuck some in, and leave others to stand tall. Finish with the olive branches and greenery.

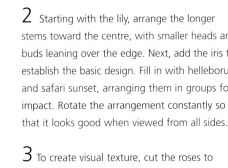

Bowl of sunshine

MATERIALS

1. Saturated gold sunflowers x 9
2. Lemons x 15
3. Egg-yolk yellow ranunculi x 20
4. Rounded glass vase

1

2

3

The bright and bold colours of this easy to arrange design will bring a smile to anyone's face and will lift the mood in a room instantly. The delicate rununculi contrast with the shape of the bright zesty lemons and the cheery sunflowers have a power all their own.

1 Fill the vase all the way to the top with lemons.

2 Using the lemons to anchor the stems, add the sunflowers around the edge and fill in the middle. Make sure the stems do not show through the lemons.

3 The ranunculi are added in groupings to fill in vacant spaces. These can be arranged in varying heights for added depth.

Tropical fun

MATERIALS

1. Splashy yellow oncidium orchids x 22
2. Umbrella ferns x 8
3. Fern fronds x 15
4. Clusters of tropical grass x 6
5. Bamboo pole approximately 36 in (1 m) long
6. Florist's bouquet holder
7. Hot glue gun

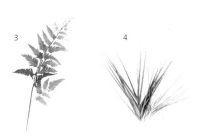

This is a great alternative to bridesmaids' bouquets for a beach wedding. Weddings can be so serious when it really should be one of the most fun days of your life. The splashy yellow oncidium orchids and fern fronds spill out playfully. Treat yourself and your guests to an experience that none of you will ever forget.

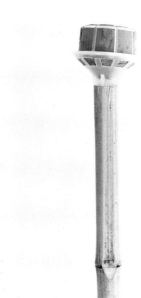

1 Cut the handle off of the bouquet holder and glue it on to the end of the bamboo stick.

2 Green the holder with umbrella fern fronds to hide the mechanics.

3 Keeping the stems long, insert the orchids into the holder so that they flair up and outwards. Fill in with tropical grass and fern fronds.

Tranquil garden

MATERIALS

1. Lotus flower water lilies x 3
2. String of pearls x 5
3. Apothecary jar or large glass bowl

Less is more. While it sounds simple, it may take some practice to apply this principle successfully. In this uncomplicated design, the tranquil ambiance of the lotus flowers are complemented by the flow of the "string of pearls" dripping peacefully over the edge of the vase.

1 Fill the bottom of the vase with a few strands of the string of pearls. Twist the stem of a water lily into a spiral and set into vase. Cut a second water lily shorter and curl the stem slightly.

2 Take a third water lily and cut the stem off. Nestle the bloom on top of the stems of the other lilies. Wrap the string of pearls around the neck of the jar and loosely twist the ends together holding them in place.

3 Repeat this around the neck of the jar in order to get multiple hanging pieces.

Chinese lantern

Shansui or "mountain water" paintings were the most prolific form of art in the Tang Dynasty of China. These landscapes were monochromatic and sparse. Their intention was capture the essence and reflect the rhythm of nature. Inspired by this single colour philosophy and the great symbolism in Chinese culture, this lantern possesses great meaning beyond its lone colour. The yellow forsythia blossoms promise of renewal, and yellow symbolizes the promise of good fortune and prosperity of the earth.

1 Fill the bottom of the lantern with pebbles or marbles to stabilize it. Insert the tallest branches first and fill in around them with medium and short branches until satisfied with the fullness.

2 Disguise the hanger wire by twisting thinner and smaller branches around it.

Cool blues

MATERIALS

1. Powder blue agapanthus x 9
2. Bee's blue delphinium x 7
3. Violet cornflowers x 18 plus 9 buds
4. Pitcher or vase

The sheer number and intricate shape of the florets on each one of these flowers gives an overall effect of abundance. An effortless gathering of wild garden and field flowers look as if you just brought them in from your cottage garden. Blues work best when shown in natural light, so place this little arrangement near your kitchen window or breakfast table.

1 Cut the stems of the agapanthus so they are approximately equal in length and place into the container at varying angles to yield a rounded shape.

2 Add the delphinium for volume and texture cut to about the same length.

3 Finish off with the cornflower and its buds to break up the blue and add depth.

Oriental style

MATERIALS

1. Japanese fatsia leaves x 4
2. Magenta phaleanopsis blooms x 6
3. Ball of sprouting vines
4. Espresso stained wooden box

1

2

3

4

The Japanese have an uncomplicated style that is like nothing else. Confidence in design, allows them to appreciate the inherent beauty in objects created both by nature and by man. The phaleanopsis orchid is arguably one of the most beautiful creations on earth. Its vibrant and pure colours are only enhanced by its exquisite shape. Paired with the organic sphere of sprouting twigs and deep green fatsia leaves, this arrangement needs only to be displayed on an appropriate pedestal.

1 Cut the stems short on the fatsia leaves. Overlap them as they are placed lying down in the box. Nestle the ball in the centre of the arrangement.

2 Cut the phaelanopsis blooms off the main stem leaving approximately an inch of stem to work with. Weave the stem of the bloom into the vines of the ball in a random fashion.

Schiaparelli-pink bouquet

MATERIALS

1. Deep coral pink floribunda garden roses x 6
2. Pale pink parrot tulips x 6
3. Vivid pink stargazer lilies x 6
4. Pink-dipped gloriosa buds x 6
5. Poke berries x 6
6. Florist's tape
7. Pink dupion ribbon in 2 shades
   2½ in (6 cm) wide x 12 in (30 cm) long and
   1 in (2.5 cm) wide x 12 in (30 cm) long
8. Faux jewels x 3
9. Pin to secure ribbon

In this bouquet of lavishly fringed parrot tulips, plump garden roses, and lilies in shades of pink, texture is achieved via the use of gloriosa buds and poke berries. For a bit of whimsy, sparkling jewels are an optional addition to dress up the bouquet. A gorgeous dupion silk ribbon in two shades of pink covers the stems and adds to the visual intricacy.

1 Gather two tulips and a rose as the central starting point. Add each additional tulip, rose, and lily to the grouping by placing its stem diagonally across the stems already held in your hand. Make sure to keep the bouquet relatively tight so as not to lose the shape of the arrangement you are building.

2 From time to time, rotate the bouquet and view it from different angles. This is to avoid missing any holes and to maintain the consistency of the desired shape.

3 Once you reach about 80 percent of your desired size, add gloriosa buds and poke berries from above and around the sides. You may have to loosen your grip slightly in order to thread the stems down into the others.

4 For visual intrigue and a bit of fun, keep
a few of the buds and berries popping out
of the bouquet at different lengths.

Glorious shades of pink with faux jewels
and dupion ribbon make this spring
bouquet playful yet elegant.

5 Once you are satisfied with the bouquet's shape and the combination of flowers, you will need to tape the stems directly under the flower heads first and then near the base. Wrap the tape tightly around a few times in order to keep the stems from shifting.

6 Fold the wider ribbon halfway along its length and place the stems in the fold. Then start at the bottom with your second colour ribbon, twisting and wrapping around the back, then toward you, continuing upward in a lacing fashion. Tie a tight knot at the top and secure with a pin.

7 Last but not least, push in the faux jewels to really make this bouquet pop!

Seasons and holidays

The changing seasons can offer so much in the way of
inspiration for design. From snow whites to the warm
colours of autumn, draw from what surrounds you or what
evokes the season for you. Holidays have their traditional
colours or designs that represent them, and here we present
them with an added twist.

Early summer garden party

MATERIALS

1. Brambling clematis vines x 12
2. Twiggy stems of spring blossom lilac x 5
3. Velvet-petalled old fashioned roses x 12
4. Glowing pink bleeding hearts x 6
5. Airy maiden hair fern x 18
6. French lavender x 18
7. Blackberry vines x 6
8. Foam
9. Papier-mâché insert
10. Antique sap bucket

Inspired by the beginning of summer when your garden is bursting with mature blooms, this unstructured collection of garden flowers reflects how they grow in nature. The brambling clematis vine and airy maiden hair fern are doing what they do artlessly.

1 Once you have inserted the foam and papier-mâché container into the sap bucket, start greening with the maiden hair fern for a loose, airy look. Next comes the clematis, arranged as you would see it in nature—brambling and loose. Tweak the blooms so they face toward you.

2 Add the lilac branches to lend visual weight to the arrangement. Play with them until they seem to bend naturally.

3 When you are satisfied with the lilac, fill in with your roses. Vary the lengths of the stems to create visual depth. In addition, play with the angles that you insert them so that some spill over the edge to most closely resemble how you might discover them in a natural garden.

4 Nature's design of the bleeding heart floret is ideal for shape variation and colour contrast to the dominating purples and blues. Keep the stems long so that they trail over the sides.

Using a distressed antique urn gives this
delightful display an old-world charm.

5 Blackberry branches are used for texture
and whimsy. Keep branches shorter so that the
berries fill in vacant spaces in the arrangement.

6 To add structure and height, insert groupings
of lavender in the centre and in open areas.

Autumn wall-hanging

MATERIALS

1. Rich green magnolia clusters x 7
2. Wispy twigs x 3
3. Chocolate sunflowers x 7
4. Pepperberry sprays in autumnal hues x 5
5. Caramel orchids x 3–5
6. Acorns x 8–10
7. Florist's tape
8. Wide ribbon
9. Green florist's wire
10. Hot glue gun

When everyone else is hanging corn husks and scarecrows on their doors you can proudly show off something that makes more of a statement. Making a departure from the expected flora, this hanging arrangement still complements the season with its display of conventional colours.

1 Cluster four or five stems of magnolia in your hand, keeping some leaves taller in the back. Tape securely into place as this will act as a sturdy base for you to build on.

2 Continue adding stems to the base and sides to create fullness and tape again. The goal is to design a triangular shaped arrangement with a flat back to hang against a wall or door.

3 Add sunflowers in a random fashion, keeping some slightly longer in the back.

4 Next insert the twigs, some of which will be longer in the back and allowing the ones on the side to naturally fan out. Occasionally hold the bouquet at arm's length to get the best perspective.

5 For visual interest insert gatherings of pepperberries in areas that are not already occupied. Tape all of the remaining stems together tightly.

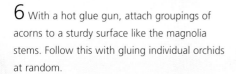

6 With a hot glue gun, attach groupings of acorns to a sturdy surface like the magnolia stems. Follow this with gluing individual orchids at random.

7 After you have trimmed the stems and wrapped them with your ribbon, form a large loose bow. Next, glue in stems of magnolia into the open end until you have hidden your mechanics.

8 To finish off, create a loop for hanging the arrangement so the flower heads hang down, with your wire at the back side. Be sure to hide it so that you can't see it when hung.

Spring flower display

MATERIALS

1. Inky purple pansies x 8
2. Delicate lilies of the valley x 3
3. Sunny daffodils x 12
4. Maiden hair fern fronds x 12
5. Galax leaves x 6
6. Moss mounds
7. Bird's nests
8. Styrofoam sheet
9. Trough
10. Blue speckled quail eggs

This type of design would be perfectly suited at home on an old farm table. The rustic wooden trough shows flowers off in their simplest form framed by mounds of moss. The inky purple pansies and delicate lilies of the valley aren't crowded by their neighboring fern fronds and sunny daffodils.

1 Place mounds of moss to completely cover the Styrofoam base. If you so desire, you can secure the moss with either wire pin staples or glue.

2 Our goal here is to create the look of a growing garden so a natural free-form approach is best. Place lily of the valley clusters in the centre and off to the sides.

3 Add the daffodils in bunches sprinkled generously throughout the moss.

4 Next, the pansies are tucked into crevices in the moss.

You can imagine that spring has truly
arrived with this lovely rustic trough.

5 To simulate a natural forest floor, the galax
leaves and fern fronds are scattered among
the flowers.

6 For visual intrigue and a bit of fun, a few
nests were added with some colourful blue
quail eggs.

Festive gift box

The rich colours of holiday festivities are brought together in this twist on a seasonal decoration. The elegant dupion silk and shimmering garnet ribbon embellishes the traditional hues of cardinal and gold, bringing warmth to a what can be a chilly time of year.

MATERIALS

1. Pomegranates with stems x 3
2. Ruby red Asiatic lilies x 7
3. Black magic roses x 6
4. Gold bay leaves x 12
5. Deep garnet hanging amaranthus 6
6. Petite calla lilies in the dark burgundy x 7
7. Pine cones x 5
8. Wide ribbon
9. Dry foam
10. Dupion silk
11. Box
12. Florist's wire
13. Hot glue gun

1

2

3

4

5

6

7

8

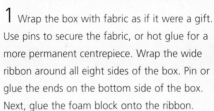

1 Wrap the box with fabric as if it were a gift. Use pins to secure the fabric, or hot glue for a more permanent centrepiece. Wrap the wide ribbon around all eight sides of the box. Pin or glue the ends on the bottom side of the box. Next, glue the foam block onto the ribbon.

2 Make a multi-looped bow, securing the loops with wire and stick them down into the centre of the foam. Secure with glue. Push a few pomegranates into the foam.

3 Hanging amaranthus is added to the lower part of the block so that it will spill over the top of the box.

4 Cover the rest of the block with the gold leaves and fill in with roses primarily located near the top.

5 Insert calla lilies into the lower half of the arrangement to allow them to arc downward. Use the Asiatic lilies for accent and position them nearer the top. Finish off your arrangement by gluing the pinecones into place.

Easter basket

MATERIALS

1. Clumps of spring grass x 2
2. Raspberry sorbet tulips x 8
3. Peachy ranunculi x 6
4. Sunny yellow daffodils x 5
5. Bird's nests x 2–3
6. Mood moss
7. Wire floral staples
8. Easter basket
9. Dry foam
10. Quail eggs
11. Hot glue gun
12. Bumblebee

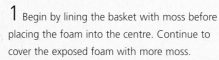

Spring grass, raspberry sorbet tulips, peachy ranunculi, and sunny yellow daffodils—what could be more seasonal? When you've outgrown sweets and chocolate bunnies, why not keep the tradition alive with this festive basket or make this as a special gift for an Easter hostess.

1 Begin by lining the basket with moss before placing the foam into the centre. Continue to cover the exposed foam with more moss.

2 Insert clumps of grass into the foam at the rear of the basket to create height.

3 Carefully glue the eggs into the nests and when dry, secure the nests with wire staples into the foam.

4 Place the second nest on the other side. Attach the bumblebee to the tall grass with the glue gun.

5 Arrange the tulips primarily in the centre of the basket keeping them tall.

This cute easter basket has eggs and a bumblebee to nod to the new beginnings of spring.

6 Daffodils are kept short and are placed at the front of the basket.

7 Tuck some rununculi together next to the grass at the rear of the basket.

Seasonal centrepiece

MATERIALS

1. Mahogany sunflowers x 6
2. Tawny brown succulents x 3
3. Brown magnolia leaves x 6
4. Ruby hanging amaranthus x 5
5. Artichokes x 5
6. Garnet Asiatic lilies x 6
7. Caramel cymbidium orchids x 5
8. Frittalaria x 5
9. Dry foam
10. Wooden picks
11. Tape
12. Container of choice

This display harnesses the seasonal majesty and theatricality that the holiday season demands—a dramatic display for any festive family table.

1 After inserting the foam and taping it securely into the container, begin greening with magnolia leaves so that you have a base to work with. The leaves should drape over the edges of the container. Manipulate the stems and leaves at random in order to replicate a more natural feel. Next, tape artichoke stems to picks and insert at random.

2 Insert succulents at the lower portions of the arrangement.

3 The sunflowers should be positioned at varying heights and angles to create depth.

4 To break up the brown, add garnet lilies at random with some loosely falling outwards and the taller ones in the centre.

5 For added interest, add hanging amaranthus around the edges. Insert the stems horizontally to yield a more natural cascade and spill onto the surface. You can either add several around the base or choose to cluster just a few in random spots.

The addition of rich red sunflowers is a little seasonal joke, and a nod to the next season in line.

5 For contrast add the petite and delicate frittalaria to offset the mass created by the larger flora.

6 Finally, tuck in a few caramel orchids in order to balance the colour palette, drawing the observer in to discover the complexity of the arrangement.

Christmas wreath

MATERIALS

1. Miniature roses in holiday red x 30–35
2. Rich cranberry coloured pomegranates with picks attached x 30–35
3. Petite pine cones x 25–30
4. Succulent red raspberry clusters x 40–50
5. Polystyrene circular wreath
6. Moss
7. Hot glue gun

Here is a blend of traditional materials with an unexpected twist. Hang on your front door to welcome guests, or use flat as a festive centrepiece with a collection of ivory or red candles.

1 Glue a light layer of moss onto the foam wreath form.

2 Place the pomegranates first as they are the largest and will help guide your placement for the items that fill in space around them.

3 Next, glue some pine cones and attach.

4 Add clusters of raspberries next to the pinecones and pomegranates.

5 Add a few roses here and there as accents. Repeat steps 2–5 until you have completely covered the wreath. For added texture and coverage, you can fill in small crevices with extra moss.

ABOUT THIS BOOK

Pregnancy is one of the most important journeys that you will ever embark upon. To help you understand as much as possible about this eventful and exciting period of your life, this book is arranged chronologically. It takes you from the moment you conceive, through each week of your pregnancy to the day of delivery, and then provides all the information you need to give birth and care for yourself and your baby afterwards. This chronological arrangement means that, as your journey through pregnancy progresses, you will be able to find your way around the relevant part of the book smoothly. I also hope that you will be able to find the answers to most – if not all – of your questions quickly and easily. Above all, I want to offer you clear, comprehensive and up-to-date information that should help you to understand the medical jargon and the experiences you may encounter in the next few months.

The "journey" section of the book is divided into the three trimesters of pregnancy. Everyone seems to have their own idea about exactly which weeks fall in each trimester so I have allowed some overlap here. The only important thing is that each one corresponds to an important and quite distinct phase of your baby's development. At the beginning of each trimester, there is a broad overview of the major milestones that occur, then it is broken down into three more detailed "through the weeks" guides. Each of these covers what happens routinely in pregnancy, including a description of your baby's development, how your own body changes, how you may be feeling both physically and emotionally, together with a section on the antenatal care you can expect to be receiving and some common concerns linked to that particular time.

"The first trimester is the crucial period when all the organs, muscles and bones of your baby are formed"

To keep things simple I am defining the age of your pregnancy and your baby as the number of weeks from your last period. The exact dates will vary depending on your menstrual cycle and when you conceived, so please don't worry about trying to tie down the details too precisely.

In this book, I have defined the first trimester of pregnancy as the period between 0 and 13 weeks for the practical reason that by the time you reach the 13th-week milestone you will probably have been booked in for your pregnancy care at an antenatal clinic at your local hospital, GP's surgery or at home. Broadly speaking, the first trimester is the crucial period when all the organs, muscles and bones of your baby are formed. During the first eight weeks we refer to the baby as an embryo, which comes from the Greek word for "newborn", in recognition of the fact that this is the stage of organ formation or organogenesis. By eight to nine weeks of pregnancy, the embryo becomes a fetus, which means "the young one", since organ formation is complete. The second trimester is taken up with consolidating all the basic structures that have developed. During this period, the fetus grows rapidly and starts to make facial expressions, swallow, hear sounds and can be felt kicking in the mother's womb. Until relatively recently, a fetus born before 28 weeks

THE JOURNEY TIMELINE

The three trimesters are divided into 4–6 week sections offering detailed information that relates to your exact stage of pregnancy.

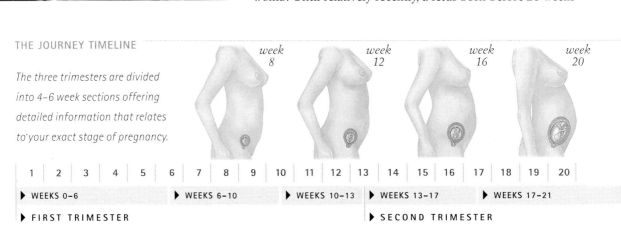

week 8   *week 12*   *week 16*   *week 20*

| 1 | 2 | 3 | 4 | 5 | 6 | 7 | 8 | 9 | 10 | 11 | 12 | 13 | 14 | 15 | 16 | 17 | 18 | 19 | 20 |

▶ WEEKS 0–6   ▶ WEEKS 6–10   ▶ WEEKS 10–13   ▶ WEEKS 13–17   ▶ WEEKS 17–21

▶ FIRST TRIMESTER   ▶ SECOND TRIMESTER

TIP

This arrangement is made in a free-form style. Rather than applying each item all at once in a single step, mix up your application of items in layers to get a more balanced finished product.

Outside-in

Every now and again it is desirable to bring a little of the outdoors
into your home. With permanent florals you are not constrained by
season, but can follow your fancy. There's a warm feeling and a bit
of fun when you can take something out of its environment and
capture its essence. In this chapter you'll find a few whimsical ideas
that will encourage you to do just that.

Poppy chair

MATERIALS

1. Brilliant orange poppies with buds x 5
2. Chocolate brown ostrich feathers x 5
3. Florist's tape
4. Chocolate brown satin ribbon

When you want to add some pizzazz to your dinner party or really make an occasion special, add some oomph to your chair backs with this refreshing approach. The brilliant orange poppies reach gracefully out of their bed of chocolate brown ostrich feathers. Tie them off with a gorgeous ribbon or sash and you are set for an alfresco feast, where ever you are.

1 Crisscross the poppy stems in your hand letting them splay out naturally.

2 Surround the stems with the feathers and tuck a few in between the centre stems.

3 Tape securely and hide the tape with ribbon. Make sure to leave the stems long to counterbalance the height of the flowers.

4 Attach the arrangement to the chair with additional ribbon keeping the tails long and stems exposed as this is part of the design.

Bird's nest

MATERIALS

1. Moss pad
2. Bird's nest
3. Spotted quail eggs x 5–7
4. Glass cloche
5. Hot glue gun

The intricate nature of bird's nests have always been a point of fascination, reminding us, as they do, of the delicate cycle of life. Using the cloche contains the subject matter and gives us cause to reflect. Natural speckled quail eggs are easily available, but you may wish to use something else more appropriate to the size of nest.

1 Simply fill your nest with eggs and glue onto the moss pad. Leave a few eggs on the pad next to the base of the nest and glue into place.

2 Cover with the cloche. Change the eggs around in the nest to refresh the arrangement.

Ocean landscape

An idyllic gathering takes on the form of a mermaid's garden in this collection of delectable succulents. The unique vessel cradles a spectrum of greens that are contrast with the glowing amber of the echevaria plant. The ferns and grasses almost seem to sway like seaweed in the underwater currents of the ocean floor. This little treasure would be perfectly at home in a bathroom or study.

MATERIALS

1. Amber hued echeveria x 1 and greenish brown echeveria x 1
2. Umbrella fern x 3
3. Jade x 1 and small succulents x 2
4. 2 clumps of wild grass
5. Coral or shell
6. Dry foam

1 Prepare the coral or shell with dry foam and start greening with the umbrella fern for impact, positioned mostly in one area.

2 Insert the wild grass toward the back since it is taller making sure that it fans outwards creating a natural backdrop.

3 Nestle the jade in between the grass and the fern.

4 Continue adding different varieties of succulents, making sure there is height and size variance.

Herbal bouquet

MATERIALS

1. Sage x 5
2. Coriander bunches x 4
3. Onion grass x 5
4. Rosemary sprigs x 3
5. Silvery-gray dusty miller with berries x 3
6. Florist's tape
7. Raffia

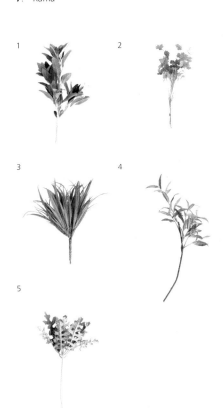

Not every bouquet has to be your run-of-the-mill mix of flowers. This gathering of delicious herbs and foliage thumbs its nose at the status quo. While perfectly suitable to carry down the aisle, you may simply want to place this in an old jam jar on your kitchen windowsill.

1 In one hand arrange a group of sage leaves and dusty miller. Use the spiral insertion technique for starting bouquets as covered in detail by the Schiaparelli-pink bouquet (page 46).

2 Add the coriander bunches in a triangular format. For the best visual balance use an odd number of bunches.

3 Fill in with rosemary and more sprigs of sage to create fullness.

4 Tuck clusters of onion grass into the bouquet for texture. When you feel the bouquet is well rounded and balanced, tape the stems at the base of the leaves and tie off with a generous bow of raffia.

Dinner party centrepiece

MATERIALS

1. Rich green magnolia leaves x 8
2. Warm cream hydrangea florets x 5
3. Variegated dahlias x 6
4. Buttery shades of ivory anemone x 10
5. Fiddlehead fern
6. Square box
7. Papier-mâché container
8. Dry foam

Perfect for a dinner party with some new friends, this arrangement is elegant without being stiff. Subtle hues of creamy pastels have been chosen so as not to take away from the beauty and impression of your food and wine. The buttery shades of ivory anemone contrast well against the rich magnolia leaves. A variegated dahlia brings in a splash of colour and the playful fiddlehead fern is sure to be a conversation starter.

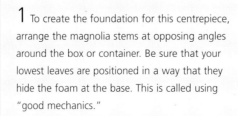

1 To create the foundation for this centrepiece, arrange the magnolia stems at opposing angles around the box or container. Be sure that your lowest leaves are positioned in a way that they hide the foam at the base. This is called using "good mechanics."

2 Insert the hydrangea starting with one in the centre and then follow with one in each corner of the box. If using a round container, make an "X" pattern with an odd number of flowers.

3 The dahlia is the second-largest flower and should be arranged in vacant areas between the hydrangea and magnolia leaves. Vary the length of the stems so that the shorter ones recess the flower to add depth to the arrangement.

4 The anemones should be inserted so that
their playful faces pop out above the rest of
the flora.

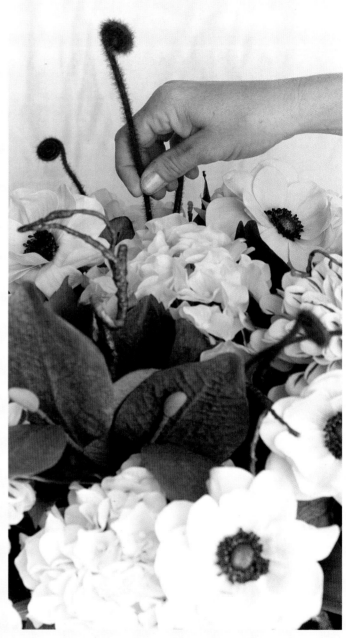

5 Fiddlehead fern adds whimsy. Randomly
place groups of two or three around the
arrangement to make more of an impact.
Fill in where necessary with magnolia stems
to complete the centrepiece.

Orchard apple crate

A great centrepiece for a kitchen table or outdoor party. This collection of vibrant fruits and flowers shows off their beauty in simplest form. The contrast of the weathered and worn crate plays off nicely with the crisp, clean lines of the fresh contents. Don't be afraid to work items like halved fruits or vegetables into your work as sometimes the insides hold more allure than the exterior.

MATERIALS

1. Deep coral pink gloriosa lilies x 5
2. Dark pink columbine florets x 12
3. Split pomegranates x 4
4. Red cherries with stems x 400
5. Mood moss
6. Antique wooden apple crate
7. Sheet of green Styrofoam

1 Gather all the materials together and place the Styrofoam in the bottom of the crate. This will anchor the flower stems and elevate the arrangement in the crate.

2 Place the split pomegranates down the centre of the crate.

TIP

The best crates are old ones with plenty of character. If you don't have one, try barn sales, flea markets, and antique shops. Happy hunting!

3 On one side of the pomegranates, tightly arrange gloriosa lilies so they are level with the fruit.

This is a real harvest festival and would look fabulous at a barbeque.

4 On the opposite side, insert columbine blooms using the same technique.

5 Cover the foam with moss on each outside edge where the cherries will go and then pour in a generous amount of cherries. Fill in the outside edges and any gaps between the fruit and flowers with extra tufts of moss.

Vineyard urn

This arrangement corrals all of the colours, dimensions, and textures of the vineyard. Integrating fruit and vegetables into the presentation is a passion —they are so beautiful on their own, so why not include them in the mix! What's great about this arrangement is that is very versatile in that it can be used for most of the year. All you need to do is change out the berries and pods according to season.

MATERIALS

1. Billowy golden sunflowers x 6
2. Sunflower buds x 6
3. Sunny yellow and brown mini-cosmos x 6
4. Mahogany magnolia leaves x 12
5. Tall onion grass x 3
6. Rich, burnt orange rosehip berries x 5
7. Merlot grape clusters x 4
8. Branches of pod bursts x 3
9. Dry foam
10. Flower picks
11. Papier-mâché container
12. Rustic urn

1 First prepare the grapes by taping the stems to wooden picks. Insert the "picked" grapes into the front side of the urn.

2 Magnolia leaves are arranged in the rear and sides to create a framework for the rest of the flora, then fill in the centre with onion grass.

3 Sunflowers are arranged in the front, off to the sides, and to the back for height. Cluster the sunflower buds at the front. Add more onion grass if necessary for volume.

4 For texture add rosehip stems and pod burst branches. The rosehip is more of a filler whereas the pod burst branches add height to the design.

5 To soften the angular lines of the sunflowers, onion grass and branches, add the mini-cosmos for their delicate and airy appearance.

Peony topiary

MATERIALS

1. Fluffy peppermint peonies x 24
2. Peony leaves x 24
3. Topiary form
4. Basket to fit form
5. Hot glue gun

The symmetry of topiary lends itself to repetition well, perhaps several along a wall or table. This quintessential topiary makes a great gift and is fun to make. The ball of fluffy peppermint peonies adds to the casual look and it's dressed-down appearance is accomplished by using a basket. For a more formal topiary, substitute a porcelain vase or cast iron urn.

1 Prepare by placing the base of the form into your basket and secure. Next, cut the peony heads off at the base of the bloom and the leaves off of the stems. Make sure to save all of the leaves for later. Using your glue gun, start gluing the peony heads at the base of the ball and work your way up and around for complete coverage. Glue in a few leaves in between the peonies for added visual interest.

2 Glue the remaining leaves in layers at the base of the topiary to create depth and hide the mechanics.

TIP

Try to select a basket or vessel that the form fits snugly into. Otherwise, secure the base of the form with crumpled newspaper.

Occasions

What better way to punctuate or celebrate a special occasion than with flowers. There is no better excuse for a dramatic gesture or a heartfelt gift. Whether it be for a silver anniversary or Valentine's Day, permanent florals will be enjoyed long after the moment. Explore some of these ideas to add some pizzazz to your, or someone else's, special occasion.

New baby carriage

MATERIALS

1. Bee's blue delphinium x 6
2. Sweets
3. Hot glue gun
4. Wire carriage

In this sweet design, the delphinium florets soften the petite wire carriage. This simple and easy to make gesture will surely be well received and enjoyed by any new mother.

1 Cut delphinium florets off their stems making sure you get open blooms and buds. Start by gluing the largest blooms around the top edge of the carriage. To cover up these stems, repeat the process on the inside edge as well. Next, completely cover the bonnet and outer edge with full, open blooms. If necessary, go back and fill in with buds.

2 Each wheel is embellished with three blooms glued together to create one flower. Attach to the centre of the wheel. Fill with sweets.

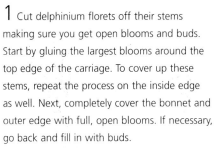

TIP

For a baby girl carriage, use pink larkspur.

Mother's day arrangement

This simple style is cheerful and elegant, perfect for the springtime. Any mother would be pleased to receive such a long-lasting gift.

MATERIALS

1. Periwinkle muscari x 18
2. Sultry magenta anemones x 12
3. Dry foam
4. Porcelain container

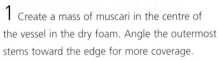

1 Create a mass of muscari in the centre of the vessel in the dry foam. Angle the outermost stems toward the edge for more coverage.

2 Completely surround the muscari with the anemones. The arrangement is finished when you can no longer see the supporting foam.

Tea party

A child's imagination can leave you bewildered and inspired. Add an adult's creativity and you can bring their fantasies to life. Have some fun and blur the boundaries between reality and fantasy. These giant tea cups will instantly bring in visions of mad hatters and chatting rabbits. Bring in a few more elements from Alice's wonderland and have a real tea party!

MATERIALS

1. Early Spring hydrangea x 6
2. Soft pink tulips x 12
3. Raspberry spider gerbera x 9
4. Creamy anemone x 6
5. Oversized teacup
6. Dry foam

1 After you have prepped your teacup with dry foam, insert the hydrangea. Use as many as are necessary for your size vessel to give the appearance of the flowers and leaves spilling over some of the edges.

2 Add the gerberas and be generous as this is such a fun and playful flower. Your goal should be to create a full and plump dome shaped gathering of flowers.

3 Tulips are added in clusters for maximum impact. In order to mimic their tendency to keep growing even after they are cut, make their heads pop out just a bit above the other flowers.

4 Anemones are added for shape variation and for their child-like flower heads.

Silver anniversary

MATERIALS

1. English Oxford roses x 12
2. Velvety lamb's ears x 12
3. Passion flower vines x 6
4. Antique silver urn
5. Dry foam
6. Papier-mâché container

There's more to this arrangement than meets the untrained eye. Besides the obvious silver container, the roses and greens echo the silver theme. The Oxford rose is a close cousin of the sterling silver rose and the velvety lamb's ear has subtle silver tones that suit the old urn nicely.

1 Put foam into papier-mâché container and place into your urn. Establish a base of lamb's ear inserted at multiple angles into the foam at varying length and height with equal coverage throughout.

2 For visual weight, add the roses. Recess some of the blooms and buds to give depth to the arrangement. If necessary, fill in open areas or "holes" with more lamb's ear.

3 Add passion flower vine so it spills out over the sides.

Valentine's heart

MATERIALS

1. Ruby red roses x 24
2. Heart-shaped polystyrene form
3. Moss
4. U-shaped wire pins

The red rose is recognized the world over as the symbol for love, and with a heart being the adopted shape of Valentine's Day how could you go wrong with this arrangement? This romantic token is guaranteed to make an impact even though it is so simple to make.

1 Prepare for this project by cutting all of the stems of the roses to about ¾ in. long and then spread the petals outward to get more coverage. Push the cut roses into the polystyrene. Start on the outside edge and work your way inward.

2 Once you have completely covered the top, cover the sides of the form with moss using the wire pins to secure it.

Bridal buttonhole

MATERIALS
1. Phaelanopsis orchid bloom x 1
2. Umbrella fern frond x 1
3. Tropical grass x 2
4. Florist's tape
5. Boutonniere pin

This straightforward and sophisticated boutonniere is ideal for a city wedding or beach ceremony. Its modern approach goes beyond the traditional rose or carnation. This would make a great buttonhole for a man, or a small corsage for a woman.

1 Place the stem of the orchid on top of a small fern frond.

2 Create a couple of loops with the grass and tape all stems into place leaving a grass tail. Insert pin into the taped portion when attaching to a lapel.

MATERIALS

1. Flowing passion vine with flowers x 3
2. Green cranberry clusters x 3
3. Geranium or other large leaf x 12
4. Decorative boxes (to resemble cake)
5. Dry foam

As cake designs are becoming more elaborate and daring, so too should the floral décor. Each approach depends on the style of the cake, this case being playful and organic. The flowing passion vine is great to use since it has a natural cascade. It spills down the cake and leads the eye to the passion flower which has great visual texture, in turn softened by the round berries.

1 Green the foam block with leaves making sure most of it is covered and add the passion vine so it tumbles naturally down the sides of the cake.

2 Fill in with berries and cut passion flowers.

3 Place clusters of berries, passion vine leaf and flowers on each tier.

4 To create visual balance, swirl some passion vine in front of the cake and off the side of the table.

Christmas bridal bouquet

MATERIALS

1. Crimson red amaryllis x 4
2. Ruby red ostrich feathers x 5
3. Wired ribbon in garnet
4. Corsage pins

Getting married around Christmas is a special event, so why not have fun with your flowers. Christmas doesn't have to be just about pinecones and evergreens. Get away from traditional styles and give the guests something to talk about. Amaryllis are a favourite around the house in the holidays for their drama as well as their fabulous colour.

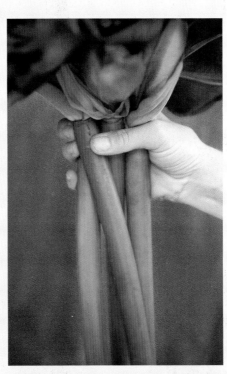

1 Gather three amaryllis stems, adding each new stem at an angle in order to form a rounded bouquet. Tape the stems into position at base of flower heads.

2 Carefully insert the feathers between the blooms in the middle of the bouquet and around the edges.

3 Secure the quills with tape and finish by wrapping stems with ribbon. Pin the ribbon ends into place and tie with a bow.

TIP

Amarylis also come naturally in shades of white. This bouquet would look equally dramatic with white feathers, flowers and white or green ribbon.

Summer cascade bridal bouquet

MATERIALS

1. Lacy green angel vines x 5
2. Bridal wreath sprays x 5
3. Fresh, crisp white phalaenopsis orchids x 6
4. Tape
5. Double-faced satin ribbon in moss green

The natural beauty of this cascading bouquet will bring confidence to the bride. This sophisticated arrangement is perfect for any wedding setting, whether it be on a beach, a field, or in a chapel. With its fresh crisp orchids, lacy green angel vine and darling bridal wreath all arcing downward as one, you can't help but notice to whoever holds it.

1 Gather the vines in one hand letting them drape naturally. Tape stems together to make handling easier as the bouquet builds in size.

2 Phalaenopsis orchids have a natural arc in real life so re-create this by tweaking on the stems before layering them in a crisscross fashion in and above the vine. Keep a couple of stems longer to create a cascade effect and keep a few stems closest to the hand for a mass of blooms.

3 Apply the same approach with the bridal spray making sure that a couple of stems are longer to add to the draping effect.

4 Pull some of the shorter strands of angel vine through to the front of the bouquet to add texture and colour. Complete the bouquet by tying off with a sumptuous ribbon keeping the ends very long.

Spring bridal bouquet

This bouquet evokes the informal gathering of spring flowers picked on a morning walk, and would be perfect for a bride, or anyone else who's in touch with nature and finds the bouquet appealing. It is a relaxed, elegant, and sophisticated arrangement—simple and sexy.

MATERIALS

1. Spring green fern fronds x 8
2. Crisp white camellias x 5
3. Sprigs of green berries x 2
4. Queen Anne's lace x 8
5. Viburnum blossoms x 7
6. Pear blossoms x 4
7. Tape
8. Grass-green wired ribbon

1 Gather the fern fronds loosely in one hand, angling the stems across one another.

2 Add camellias one at a time in a spiral around the base of the fern and slightly off-centre.

3 The berries are added next in a triangular pattern. Make sure not to push them too far into the bouquet as there are more flowers to come.

TIP

This is an informal gathering of spring blooms so be sure to keep your grip loose while arranging.

4 The viburnum surrounds the base of the bouquet like a cuff adding extra dimension and fullness.

Inspired by nature, this spring bouquet
could be replicated in smaller bunches
for bridesmaids and buttonholes.

5 Fill in open spaces with Queen Anne's lace.

6 Last but not least, add the pear blossoms to
the centre and outer edges. Wrap securely with
tape and cover your stems with ribbon.

Autumn bridal bouquet

MATERIALS

1. Brilliant orange garden roses x 6
2. Caramel cymbidium orchids x 7
3. Tawny brown magnolia clusters x 3
4. Rosehip sprigs x 3
5. Garnet hanging amaranthus x 3
6. Wooden picks
7. Tape
8. Terracotta wired ribbon

Imagine scooping up a bunch of leaves and cuttings that an autumn wind blew to your feet. These rich burnt oranges and almost toffee-like hues vibrate against mahogany foliage in this maze of textures. To bring some more colour to the mix, garnet coloured amaranthus hang like rich velvet curtains. This bouquet will appeal to the bride getting married in a vineyard or rustic setting. Enjoy!

1 Hold the magnolia stems in one hand crisscrossing the stems to create a dome shaped gathering of leaves. Massage the leaves to mimic the natural effect of nature.

2 Now add roses one at a time in a spiral fashion around the base of the magnolia cluster to form a collar of roses.

3 Cut the cymbidium blooms off their stems. We do this because in reality the blooms grow 8–10 on a stem. By taping each stem to a wooden pick we create individual "flowers." Poke these orchid stems into the centre of the bouquet. Nestle each bloom far enough down so that the magnolia leaves are still visible.

From country rosehips to hothouse
orchids, these brilliant autumn shades
work together to create bold impact.

4 For texture, add rosehip berries in between the orchids making sure they are spread out in naturally in a liberal fashion as not to appear clumped together.

5 Finally, add hanging amaranthus around the base of the bouquet so it drapes down the hand that holds it or the base it's placed on.

6 Finish by taping a 4–6 in (10–15 cm) section of the stems and tightly wrap your ribbon down the length of the stems.

Faux flower stockists

Silk flowers can be found at most good craft stores. The following selection of stores offer a good range and are available to purchase online.

US

Natural Decorations, Inc. (NDI)
777 Industrial Park Drive
Brewton, Alabama 36427
www.ndi.com

BudToBlooms.com
602 North Front Street
Liverpool, PA 17045
www.budtoblooms.com

Amazon Foliages
9208 James Ave. South – Suite 7
Bloomington, MN 55431
Tel 952-884-1210
www.amazonfoliages.com

Arteflorum
111 Kimball Way
South San Francisco, CA 94080
Tel 800-755-2800
www.arteflorum.com

Silk Gardens
7709 NW 46th Street
Miami, FL 33166
Tel 305 406-0102
www.silkgardens.com

Silk Trees, Silk Plants, Silk Flowers
29 Mine Brook Road
Far Hills, NJ 07931
Tel 88-532-0232
www.artificialplantsandtrees.com

Silkflowers.com
12021 Centron Place
Cincinnati, OH 45246
1-800-783-9966
www.silkflowers.com

Silk Flowers
29 Mine Brook Road
Far Hills, NJ 07931
Tel 888-532-0232
www.silkflowers.net

UK

ArtPlants.co.uk
PO Box 5953
Wimborne, BH21 9AB
Tel 01202 810919
www.artplants.co.uk

Peony Direct
Hamilton House
Fairfax Road, Heathfield
Newton Abbot TQ12 6UD
Tel 0870 420 4959
www.peonydirect.co.uk

Silk Flowers Boutique
28 Park Grange Mount
Sheffield, South Yorks S2 3SQ
Tel 07785298067
www.silkflowersboutique.co.uk

Just Artificial
Unit 35A,Heysham Business Park,
Middleton Road, Heysham,
Lancashire, LA3 3PP
Tel 01524 858888
www.justartificial.co.uk

Bloom
Unit 3, Longhedge Lane
Bottesford, Nottinghamshire
NG13 0BF
Tel 01949 845444
www.bloom.uk.com

Fake Landscapes
64 Old Brompton Road
London, SW5 0BA
Tel 020 7835 1500
www.fake.com

Lavenders of London
Unit 12, The Metro Centre
St Johns Road, Isleworth
Middx, TW7 6NJ
Tel 0208 568 5733
www.lavendersoflondon.com

Withycombe Fair
1 Kilbury, Northfield Road
Minehead, Somerset, TA24 5QQ
Tel 01643 706355
www.withycombefair.co.uk

Carnmeal Cottage
Carnmeal Downs, Breage
Helston, Cornwall, TR13 9NL
Tel 01326 572901
www.carnmeal.com

Acknowledgements

I am who I am because of some very special people in my life. This book would not be possible without them. First and foremost, my husband and best friend Scot and our ever-patient and adoring daughter Bijou. Since I met Scot, he has made everything possible for me, my dreams and aspirations have been fulfilled through constant encouragement.

My mum, Rita, who gifted me seed money so I could embark on this business venture and pursue new avenues. My dad, Erik, has inspired me to constantly push the envelope, break the rules and be a bit of a rebel. He is a talented and renowned photographer who shot the first series of images, which lead me to be "discovered". Sande, my mother-in-law, who taught me the basic principles of floral design.

Allyson Magda, was a huge part of this project, we shared many silly giggling sessions working together and forged a stronger friendship. Last but not least, Hilton, our sprightly Rhodesian Ridgeback who has missed out on her long daily walks in order for us to complete the book.

Index

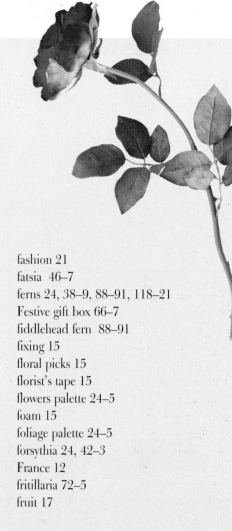

accessories 16–17
acorns 58–61
agapanthus 44–5
amaranthus 66–7, 72–5, 122–5
amaryllis 114–15
anemones 30–3, 88–91, 103, 104–5
angel vine 116–17
Aqua Casting 15
artichokes 72–5
artistic style 19
Autumn bridal bouquet 122–5
Autumn wall-hanging 58–61

baubles 17
bay leaves 66–7
bird's nests 62–5, 68–71, 82–3
blackberry vines 54–7
bleeding heart 54–7
bolt cutters 14, 15
Bowl of sunshine 36–7
branches 17
Bridal bouquets
  Autumn 122–5
  Christmas 114–15
  Spring 118–21
  Summer cascade 116–17
Bridal buttonhole 110–11
bumblebee 68–71
bunching style 19

Cake decoration 112–13
camellias 118–21
cascading style 19
cherries 30–3, 92–5
Cherry red 30–3
China 12
Chinese lantern 42–3
Christmas bridal bouquet 114–15
Christmas wreath 76–7
cleaning 13

clematis 54–7
colour wheel 21
colour(s) 20–1
  arrangements for 30–51
  complementary 21
  design and 20–1
  fashion 20, 21
  mellow arrangement 34–5
  mood and 29–51
  palette 24–5
columbines 92–5
conservative setting 27
containers 22–3
Cool blues 44–5
coral 84–5
coriander 86–7
cornflower 44–5
cosmopolitan setting 27
cosmos 96–7
cottage setting 27
coxcomb 30–3
cranberries 112–13
cutting 15
cymbidium 72–5, 122–5

daffodils 24, 62–5, 68–71
dahlia 88–91
delphiniums 44–5, 102
design colour concepts 20–1
  containers 22–3
  influences 26–7
  styles and principles 18–19
Dinner party centrepiece 88–91
dried materials 12
  maintenance 13
dusty miller 86–7

Easter basket 68–71
echeveria 84–5
equipment 14–15

fashion 21
fatsia 46–7
ferns 24, 38–9, 88–91, 118–21
Festive gift box 66–7
fiddlehead fern 88–91
fixing 15
floral picks 15
florist's tape 15
flowers palette 24–5
foam 15
foliage palette 24–5
forsythia 24, 42–3
France 12
fritillaria 72–5
fruit 17

galax 62–5
Garden party 54–7
geranium leaves 112–13
gerbera 30–3, 104–5
gloriosa lilies 48–51, 92–5
glue gun 14, 15
grapes 96–7
grasses, tropical 38–9, 68–71,
  84–5, 110–11

helleborus 34–5
Herbal bouquet 86–7
history 12
holidays arrangements for 52–77
hydrangea 88–91, 104–5

Index

iris 34–5
Italy 12

jade 83–4
Japan 12

kangaroo paws 24
knives 14

lamb's ear 106–7
lavender 54–7
lemons 36–7
leucadendron 34–5
lilac 54–7
lilies 34–5, 48–51, 66–7, 72–5
lily of the valley 62–5

magnolia 58–61, 72–5, 88–91, 96–7, 122–5
maidenhair fern 54–7, 62–5
maintenance 13
marbles 17
Marie Antoinette 12
materials 11–17
Mellow colours 34–5
monochrome style 21
mood 21
    arrangements for 30–51
    colour and 27–51
mood boards 21
moss 17
moss balls 17
Mother's day arrangement 103
muscari 103

natural style 19
New baby carriage 102

occasions arrangements for 100–25
Ocean landscape 84–5

oncidium 38–9
onion grass 86–7, 96–7
Orchard apple crate 92–5
orchids 24, 38–9, 46–7, 58–61, 72–5, 110–11, 116–17, 122–5
Oriental style 46–7
ostrich feathers 80–1, 114–15

palette 24–5
pansies 62–5
passion flower vine 106–7, 112–13
pear blossom 118–21
peonies 98–9
Peony topiary 98–9
pepperberry 58–61
permanent botanicals 12–13
phalaenopsis 46–7, 110–11, 116–17
pine cones 76–7
poke berries 48–51
pomegranates 66–7, 76–7, 92–5
poppies 80–1
Poppy chair 80–1

quail eggs 62–5, 82–3
Queen Anne's lace 118–21

ranunculi 36–7, 68–71
raspberries 76–7
ribbons 15
rigid style 19
rosehips 96–7, 122–5
rosemary 86–7
roses 30–3, 34–5, 48–51, 54–7, 66–7, 76–7, 106–7, 108–9, 122–5
rustic setting 27

sage 86–7
scents 15
Schiaparelli-pink bouquet 48–51
scissors 14, 15

seasons 26, 27
    arrangements for 52–77
Seasonal centrepiece 72–5
settings 26–7
silks 12–13
    cleaning 13
    maintenance 13
    materials for 12
Silver anniversary 106–7
Spring bridal bouquet 118–21
Spring flower display 62–5
stakes 15
staples 15
stones 17
string of pearls 40–1
succulents 72–5, 84–5
Summer cascade bridal bouquet 116–17
sunflowers 36–7, 58–61, 72–5, 96–7
sweets 102

Tea party 104–5
texture 24
tools 14–15
Tranquil garden 40–1
Tropical fun 38–9
tulips 48–51, 68–71, 104–5
twig balls 17

umbrella fern 38–9, 84–5, 110–11

Valentine's heart 108–9
vegetables 17
viburnum 118–21
Vineyard urn 96–7

water droplets 15
water lilies 40–1
wire cutters 14, 15

(HPL)